ENVIRONMENTAL ISSUES

CLIMATE CHANGE

By Harriet Brundle

PUBLISHING

Published in 2020 by
KidHaven Publishing, an Imprint of Greenhaven Publishing, LLC
353 3rd Avenue
Suite 255
New York, NY 10010

Edited by: Kristy Holmes
Designed by: Danielle Rippengill

Cataloging-in-Publication Data

Names: Brundle, Harriet.
Title: Climate change / Harriet Brundle.
Description: New York : KidHaven Publishing, 2020. | Series: Environmental issues | Includes glossary and index.
Identifiers: ISBN 9781534530706 (pbk.) | ISBN 9781534530331 (library bound) | ISBN 9781534531659 (6 pack) | ISBN 9781534530669
(ebook)
Subjects: LCSH: Climatic changes--Juvenile literature. | Climatic changes--Effect of human beings on--Juvenile literature. | Global
warming--Juvenile literature.
Classification: LCC QC903.15 B78 2020 | DDC 363.738'74--dc23

Printed in the United States of America

CPSIA compliance information: Batch #BS19KL: For further information contact Greenhaven Publishing LLC,
New York, New York at 1-844-317-7404.

Please visit our website, www.greenhavenpublishing.com. For a free color catalog of all our
high-quality books, call toll free 1-844-317-7404 or fax 1-844-317-7405.

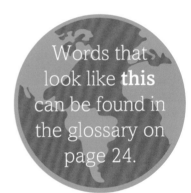

Words that look like **this** can be found in the glossary on page 24.

Photo credits: Abbreviations: l–left, r–right, b–bottom, t–top, c–center, m–middle.
Images are courtesy of Shutterstock.com. With thanks to Getty Images, Thinkstock Photo and iStockphoto.
Cover – ImagePixel. 1 – WIBOON WIRATTHANAPHAN. 2 – photolinc. 3 – kirillov alexey. 4 – Anton Petrus. 5 – Quick Shot. 6 – Li Hui
Chen. 6br – Yvonne Pijnenburg–Schonewille. 7 – Piyaset. 8 – Meryll. 9 – Anastasiia Tymoshenko. 10 – tigristiara. 11 – Mikadun.
12 – ssuaphotos. 14 – Grisha Bruev. 15 – lowsun. 17 – LifetimeStock. 18 – Sawat Banyenngam. 19 – solarseven. 20 – Anticiclo.
21 – buttchi 3 Sha Life. 22l – LZ Image. 22br – tale. 23l– yalayama. 23br – aperturesound.

CONTENTS

WHAT DOES CLIMATE MEAN?

The climate of a place is the type of weather that place usually has. The climate is the usual weather across a large area, such as a country, continent, or even the whole world.

THE CLIMATE IN THIS DESERT IS HOT AND DRY.

This is different from weather. Weather can change a lot in a single day, or even within a small area. Climate stays the same for a long period of time.

THE CLIMATE HERE IS WARM AND WET.

WHAT IS CLIMATE CHANGE?

Climate change is when the climate of a place is changing from what is usually expected.

THE CLIMATE IN THE ARCTIC IS CHANGING, CAUSING THE ICE TO MELT.

Climate change can cause the **temperature** of an area to rise or fall. It can cause more or less rain than usual, making an area much wetter or drier than we would usually expect.

GLOBAL WARMING

The average temperature of the Earth is getting warmer. This is called global warming. Even though the overall temperature rise is small, it is having very big effects.

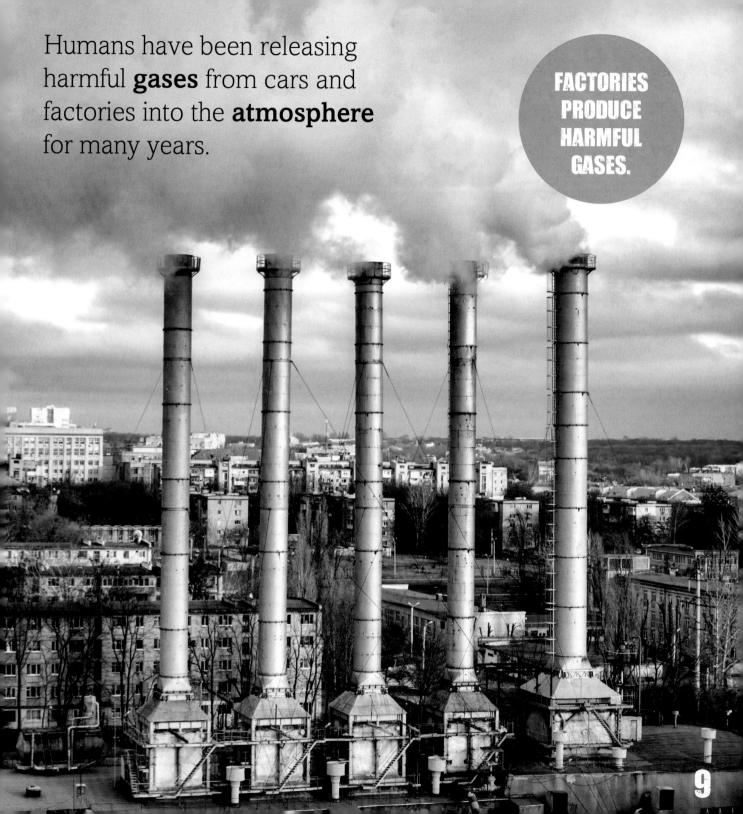

Humans have been releasing harmful **gases** from cars and factories into the **atmosphere** for many years.

FACTORIES PRODUCE HARMFUL GASES.

POLLUTION

WATER
POLLUTION

There are lots of different types of pollution. Pollution is when something harmful, like a gas or a poison, gets into the environment.

Pollution can affect every part of the environment, such as the air we breathe, the water we drink, and the soil we use to grow our food.

SOIL POLLUTION

When we burn fossil fuels to power cars and factories, they give off harmful gases that cause air pollution.

AIR POLLUTION

CARS BURN GASOLINE, WHICH IS MADE FROM FOSSIL FUEL, TO WORK.

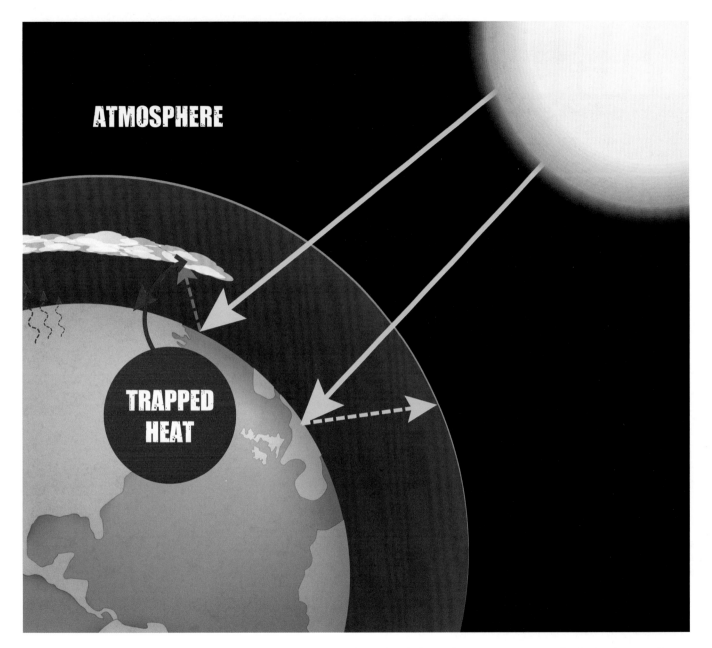

These harmful gases create a thick blanket around the Earth, trapping more heat in the atmosphere. This is called the greenhouse effect.

FARMING AND LAND USE

Trees are very important to the environment. They absorb harmful gases and make oxygen, which people and animals need to live. This helps lower air pollution.

In order to grow crops and keep animals for our food, farmers often clear large areas of forest and trees. This means trees can't do their job of lowering pollution, and it gets worse.

LARGE AREAS OF FOREST ARE CLEARED FOR FARMING EVERY YEAR.

THE ICE CAPS

The Arctic and the Antarctic are large areas of ice and frozen sea, known as the ice caps.

THE
ARCTIC

THE
ANTARCTIC

THE ICE CAPS ARE MELTING BECAUSE OF CLIMATE CHANGE.

Global warming is causing the ice caps to melt. This means that the **habitats** of the animals that live there are at risk. It also means the seas are rising, which can cause flooding.

HOW CLIMATE CHANGE AFFECTS US

Climate change has a big effect on human life. It makes the weather more extreme, which can cause problems like **droughts**, floods, large storms, and heat waves.

THIS CAN AFFECT THE AMOUNT OF FOOD WE CAN GROW.

Extreme weather can be very dangerous and make life difficult for people who live in certain areas. Tornadoes, hurricanes, and large storms become more common as the climate changes.

TORNADO

If animals and other life cannot **adjust** fast enough to climate change, they will be in danger of dying out. If this happens, we say they have become endangered.

TURTLES CAN START THEIR MIGRATION AT THE WRONG TIME IF THE SEAS ARE TOO WARM.

Coral has been badly affected by climate change. When it gets too warm, it turns white. We call this "bleaching." Many animals live in the coral and this means they are also at risk.

HOW CAN WE HELP?

Plant More Plants
Can you grow your own food in your garden? Perhaps your school could plant some trees.

Travel Smart
Walk or ride your bike instead of taking the car. Use public transportation for longer trips.

Spread the Word

Tell people what you have learned about climate change, and let them know how they can help.

Reduce, Reuse, Recycle

Find out what can be recycled, and don't throw things away if you can still use them for something else. For example, could an old jar become a pencil holder?

THERE ARE LOTS OF THINGS WE CAN DO TO HELP!

GLOSSARY

adjust slightly change to fit in or adapt better

atmosphere the mixture of gases that make up the air and surround the Earth

droughts long periods of very little rainfall, which lead to a lack of water

gases air-like substances that expand freely to fill any space available

habitats the natural environments in which animals or plants live

temperature how hot or cold something is

INDEX